KIDZBIZ

FESTIVE FUN

Gillian Souter

Off the Shelf Publishing

BEFORE YOU START...

There are special days to celebrate all through the year - these are good times to make decorations for your home and gifts for people you love. You might even discover some extra festive occasions that you can add to the calendar!

There are lots of pictures in this book to give you ideas for projects, but it's fun to make up your own designs and patterns.

For some projects you might need an adult's help, especially when you want to use a sharp knife or to bake something in the oven.

First published in 2001 by
Off the Shelf Publishing
32 Thomas Street
Lewisham NSW 2049
Australia

Projects, text and layout
copyright © 2001 Off the Shelf Publishing
Line illustrations by Clare Watson
Photographs by Andre Martin

Contents

Let's Celebrate!

There are lots of festive occasions that we celebrate around the world and throughout the year.

Chinese New Year is celebrated later than the calendar new year.

It's traditional to welcome in the new year with lots of noise!

Valentine's Day is the time to show people you love that you're thinking of them.

During Passover, Jewish people celebrate the idea of freedom.

Easter is when we celebrate new beginnings.

April Fool's Day is a great day for fun and practical jokes.

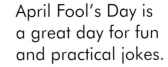

In the northern half of the world, May Day is a summer holiday.

Halloween is the evening when all the spooky things are supposed to come out!

The Jewish holiday of Hannukah is known as the 'Holiday of Lights'.

Thanksgiving and Harvest festivals celebrate the world of nature.

Ramadan is a great festival of the Islamic faith.

Kwanzaa is a festival enjoyed by people of African descent.

Lots of people around the world enjoy Christmas.

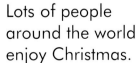

5

New Year Noise

People used to make noise at New Year to frighten away the bad spirits of the old year. Now we do it just for fun!

1 Thread a small bell onto each end of a pipe cleaner. Bend the wire to hold the bells in place. Add bells to four more pipe cleaners.

2 Bend the pipe cleaners in half and arrange them around one end of a pencil.

3 Wrap tape tightly around the pencil so that all the pipe cleaners are fixed in place.

4   To make the shaker, put
a few spoonfuls of dry
rice in a paper or plastic cup.

5   Tape another cup on top and
then decorate the shaker with
felt pens.

Now you're
ready to see in
the New Year!

Dancing Dragon

YOU WILL NEED

an egg carton
cardboard tubes
paints
a paintbrush
felt or fabric
glue
scissors
crêpe paper
tape
dowel

Celebrate Chinese New Year
by making this wonderful puppet.

1 Cut an egg carton in half.
From one half, cut two cups
to make eyes and glue them
on top of the other half.

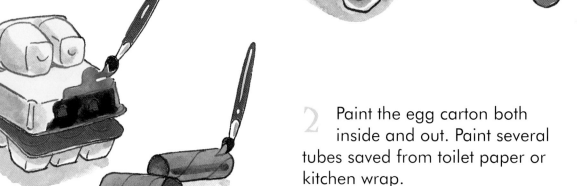

2 Paint the egg carton both
inside and out. Paint several
tubes saved from toilet paper or
kitchen wrap.

3 Cut strips of crêpe paper to
make streamers. Tape a bunch
in the middle with tape and then
stick it inside a tube. Repeat for
each tube.

4 Tape bunches of streamers onto the head.

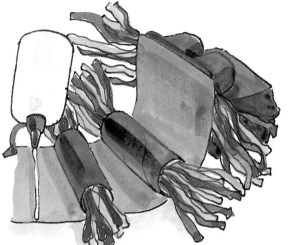

5 Glue the head and tubes onto a strip of felt or other fabric.

6 Make a hole in the base of the head and tail with the scissors. Push in two pencils or pieces of dowel.

Hold the sticks and make the dragon dance above you.

Be My Valentine

Send a pop-up heart card to someone you love.

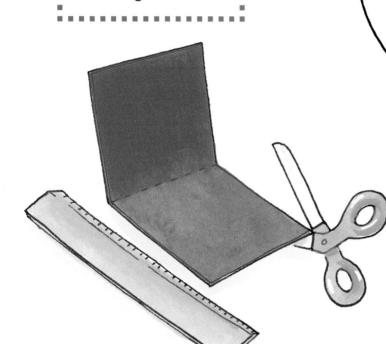

1   Measure and cut a 21 x 10.5 cm rectangle on a piece of thin card. Fold it in half to make a square shape.

2   Trace the heart pattern and cut out the tracing. Draw around it on another piece of thin card. Cut out this heart and decorate one side with glitter-glue, stickers or felt pens.

3 Cut a 10 x 2 cm strip of card and fold it in half. Now make another fold 2 cm from each end as shown.

4 Glue the strip onto the back of the heart as shown.

5 Lay the heart face down inside the card and put glue on each of the end tabs. Turn down the bottom tab. Close the card and press; when you open it the heart should pop up.

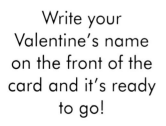

Write your Valentine's name on the front of the card and it's ready to go!

11

Paper-&-Pin Heart

Pricked paper hearts like these have been made and given for hundreds of years.

1 Fold a piece of white paper and draw half a heart along the fold.

2 Cut out the doubled paper with pinking shears or fancy scissors.

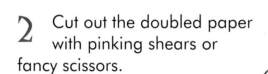

3 Wrap tape around a large needle to make a handle. Lay the heart on scrap cardboard and prick a pattern with the needle.

4 Gently glue the heart onto coloured card. Cut neatly around the paper, leaving room for a hole at the top.

5 Make a hole at the top of the heart and thread a narrow ribbon through it. Tie a bow, or knot the ribbon to make a hanging loop.

Try using this method to make other shapes too.

Passover Pocket

At Jewish Passover, someone hides a piece of matzo bread called the afikomen and everyone searches for it. Why not make an afikomen pouch?

YOU WILL NEED

felt
a ruler
scissors
pins
a needle & thread
glue
sequins
a small treat

1   Measure and cut a 29 x 10 cm rectangle of coloured felt.

2   Fold one end of the felt over by 10 cm and pin the two layers together at each side.

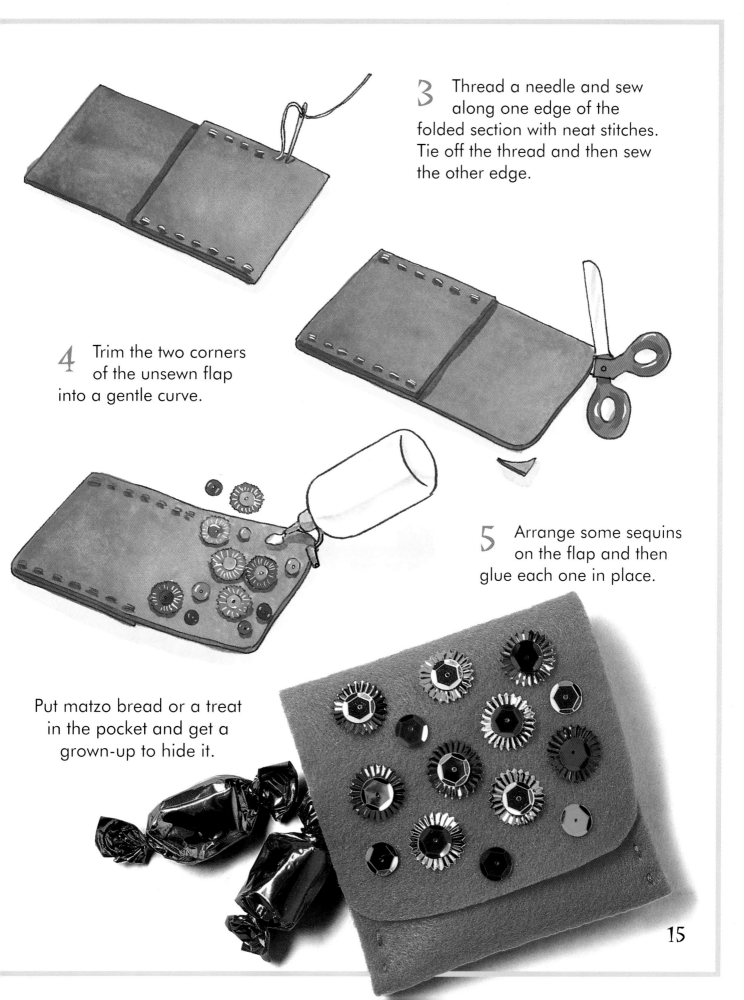

3 Thread a needle and sew along one edge of the folded section with neat stitches. Tie off the thread and then sew the other edge.

4 Trim the two corners of the unsewn flap into a gentle curve.

5 Arrange some sequins on the flap and then glue each one in place.

Put matzo bread or a treat in the pocket and get a grown-up to hide it.

Speckled Eggs

Eggs which have been blown keep for years. Make sure you get all the egg out or it will smell terrible by the end of Easter!

YOU WILL NEED

eggs
a pin
a skewer
a bowl
kitchen paper
acrylic paint
a paintbrush
a kitchen sponge
clear varnish

1 Make a hole in the top and bottom of an egg with a pin. Carefully poke in a skewer to make the holes larger and to break up the yolk.

2 Blow all the contents of the egg into a bowl. If this is difficult, make the holes a bit larger.

3 Rinse out the egg by holding it under water and then blowing through it again. When the contents are clear, drain the egg on kitchen paper.

4 Paint one half of the egg with acrylic paint. When it is dry, paint the other half.

5 Put a different colour of paint on a plastic lid. Dab a sponge or a ball of crumpled paper in the paint and then onto the egg. When it is dry, brush on a coat of varnish.

Gold paint adds a special touch, but other colours will look good too.

Chicks in the Nest

These charming chicks will bring a smile to everyone's face at Easter.

yellow food dye
cotton balls
tweezers
scrap newspaper
scissors
orange pipe cleaner
beads or felt pens
glue
an egg carton
crêpe paper

1 Add five or six drops of yellow food dye to a quarter glass of water. Drop in a cotton ball, then lift it out with tweezers. It should be bright yellow: if not, add more dye.

2 Dye each cotton ball one at a time and place them on a folded newspaper to dry overnight. You need two balls for each chick.

3 Gently pull the balls back into shape. Cut and bend small pipe cleaner beaks and glue them onto the heads.

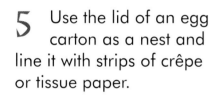

4 Glue small beads on for eyes, or draw them on with a felt pen. Glue a head onto each body.

5 Use the lid of an egg carton as a nest and line it with strips of crêpe or tissue paper.

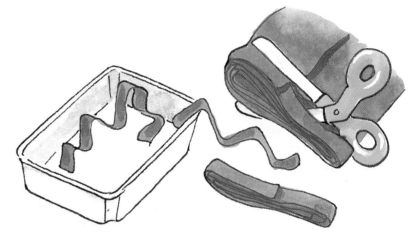

Arrange the chicks in the nest and have a happy Easter!

19

April Fool!

The 1st of April is a day for harmless tricks and jokes. These jumping jacks are just right for the occasion.

1 Cut a piece of drinking straw so that the bend is in the middle. If you don't have bendy straws, roll a square of paper tightly, glue down the edge and bend it in the middle.

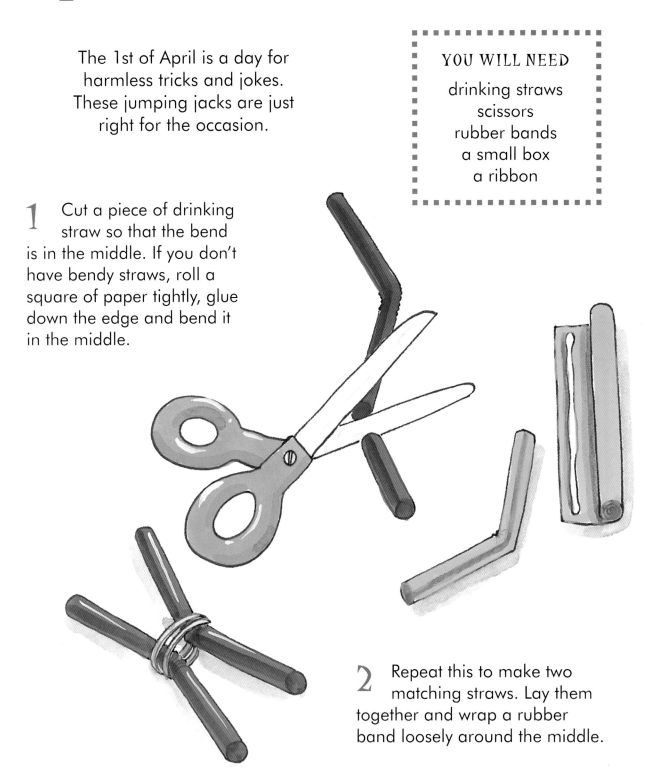

2 Repeat this to make two matching straws. Lay them together and wrap a rubber band loosely around the middle.

20

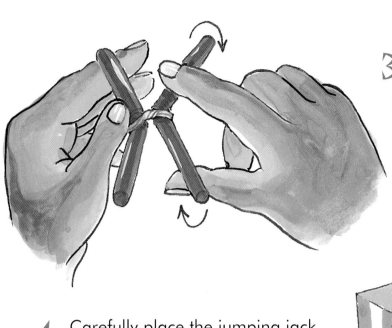

3 Wind up the jack by turning one straw as many times as possible while you hold the other one.

4 Carefully place the jumping jack in a small box and close the lid. Open the box to test that the jack jumps out as it should. Pack the box again and tie a ribbon around it.

Now offer the box to a friend and watch what happens!

Flower Power

May Day is a time for flowers and fun. Here's a way to make your own!

1 Lay a jar lid on a piece of fabric and draw around it with a pencil.

2 Cut out the circle with pinking shears. You will need three circles for each flower.

3 Thread the needle with a doubled thread and tie a knot in the end. Sew a ring of stitches around the fabric circle as shown.

4 Pull the thread and gather the fabric to make a petal. Knot the thread to hold the shape.

5 Sew three gathered petal sections together to make a full flower.

You could sew the flowers onto a hat or onto a headband like this one.

23

Pumpkin Head

No Halloween costume is complete wihout a mask. Here's one idea - you might have another scary face in mind!

1 Hold a paper plate to your face. Place two fingers over your eyes and then use a pencil to mark eye holes on the back of the plate.

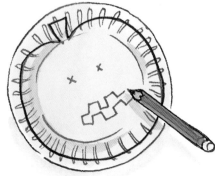

2 Use a pencil to draw a pumpkin shape on the plate.

3 Colour the pumpkin face with felt pens.

24

4 Use the point of a compass
   or a knitting needle to make
eye holes. Punch another hole
at either side of the face.

5 Tie a piece of string to
   one side. Try on the mask
to check the fit before you tie
the other side.

Now you're all set
to trick or treat.

Spider-on-a-String

YOU WILL NEED

an egg carton
scissors
a skewer
paint
a paintbrush
pipe cleaners
elastic cord
tape

Halloween is about all those creepy things that go bump in the night - here's one of them!

1 Cut a single cup from an egg carton. Use a skewer to carefully punch a hole in the top of a cup and to make eight holes around the sides.

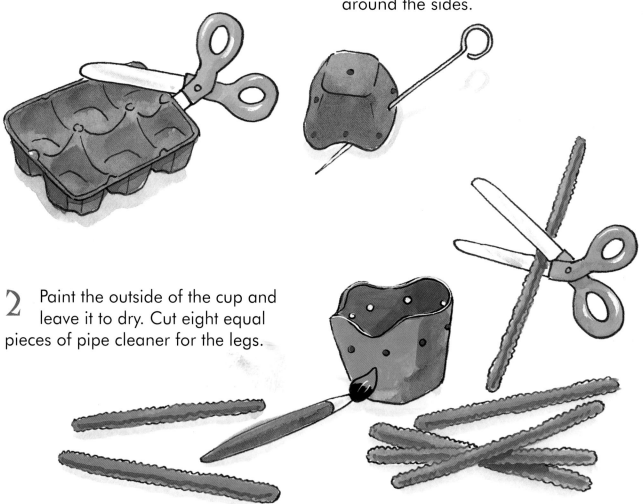

2 Paint the outside of the cup and leave it to dry. Cut eight equal pieces of pipe cleaner for the legs.

26

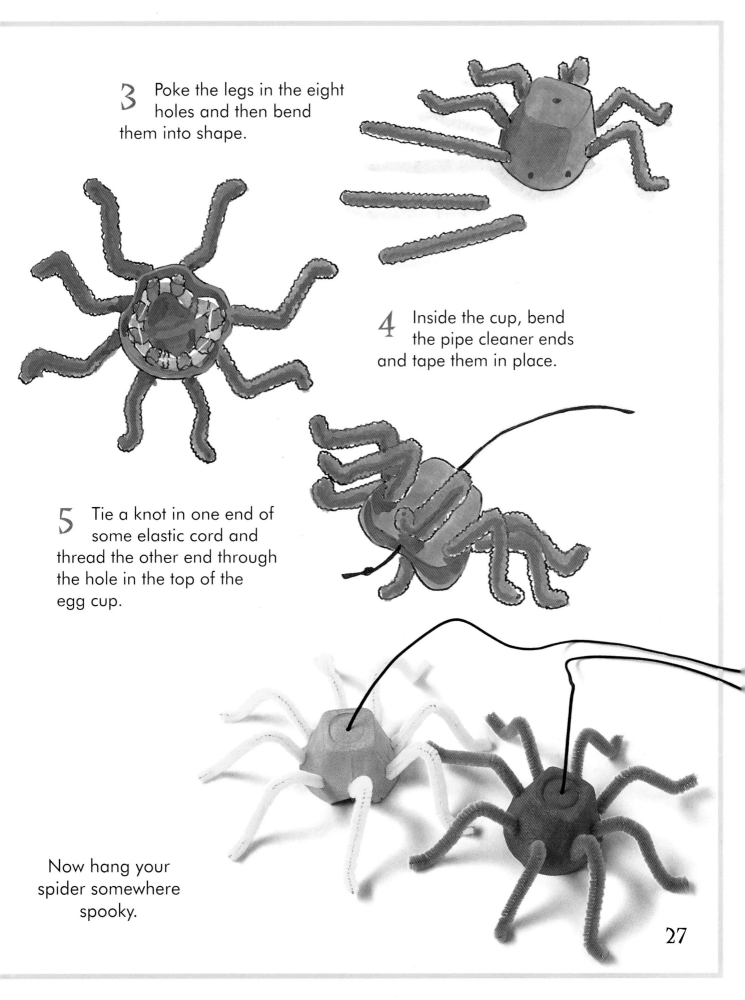

3 Poke the legs in the eight holes and then bend them into shape.

4 Inside the cup, bend the pipe cleaner ends and tape them in place.

5 Tie a knot in one end of some elastic cord and thread the other end through the hole in the top of the egg cup.

Now hang your spider somewhere spooky.

27

Spooky Shades

These candle shades will cast an eerie glow over the Halloween dinner table.

1 Cut each end off a clean plastic bottle by making a hole with a craft knife and then using scissors. This should give you a clear tube.

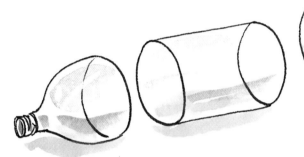

2 Mix powder paint with water. Paint the inside of the tube with a thin coat of paint and leave it to dry.

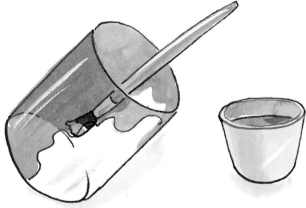

3 Draw bats, cats or other Halloween shapes on paper and fill them in with a black felt pen. Cut out the shapes.

28

4 Cut two strips of black paper or thin card and glue them around the top and bottom of the tube.

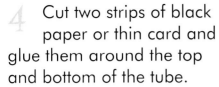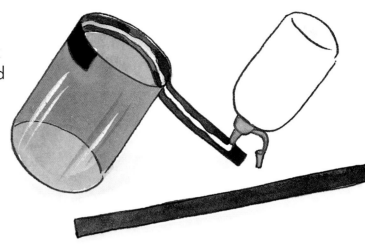

5 Glue the black shapes inside the plastic tube. Place a small candle in a clean glass jar.

Put the shade over the candle after you have lit it.

Fruity Fun

Celebrate Thanksgiving or Harvest by making fridge magnets out of salt dough.

1 Mix ½ cup of plain flour with ¼ cup of salt in a bowl. Add ¼ cup water, a little at a time, until you have a soft dough. Knead this with your hands until the dough is smooth.

2 Roll a spoonful of dough into a ball and flatten it with your palm to make large fruit. Do the same with a teaspoonful of dough for smaller fruit. Pinch leaves with your fingers.

3 Mark leaf veins with a knife. Make spots on berries and oranges with a skewer. Stick dough pieces together with a dab of water.

4 Set the oven to 120°C/ 250°F/Gas mark ½. Carefully place the finished fruit on an oven tray and bake them for 3 hours.

5 Let the dough shapes cool, then paint them with watercolours. When they are dry, brush on some clear varnish.

6 Glue a small magnet onto the back of each shape.

For a bolder effect, use bright acrylic paints instead of watercolours.

Nature's Stamp

At Thanksgiving or harvest time, you could use fruit and vegetables to make wrapping paper or stunning pictures.

1   Ask a grown-up to cut fruit and vegetables in half with a sharp knife. Wipe the cut side with a kitchen towel.

2   Mix up thick paints by adding some water to powder paint. Brush paint on the lid of a spare plastic container.

3 Press the cut side of the fruit onto the paint, wiggle it around and press it firmly on a sheet of paper.

4 Repeat step 3 to make as many prints as you like. Try making a pattern with different shapes and colours.

For extra interest, you could brush thin paint over the whole sheet of paper before printing.

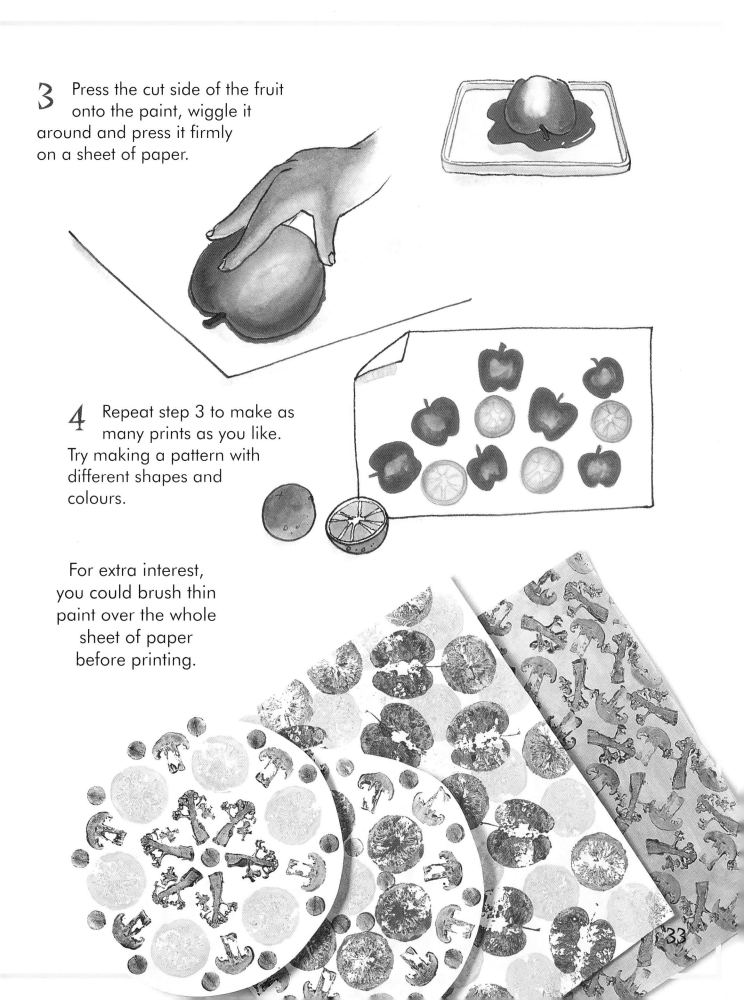

33

Dreidels

Hanukkah or Chanukah is celebrated with chocolate coins and dreidels - four-sided spinning tops.

YOU WILL NEED

air-drying clay
a ruler
a knife
thin dowel
a fretsaw
acrylic paint
a paintbrush
a metallic pen
clear varnish

1 Knead a ball of clay until it is smooth. Roll it into a sausage and flatten the sides with a ruler to make a long box shape.

2 Use a knife to cut a V-shape near one end of the clay.

3 Turn the clay so that the V-shape is on its side. Carefully cut another V-shape to form a point.

4 Make a straight cut across the clay for the top of the dreidel. Smooth all the corners with a damp finger.

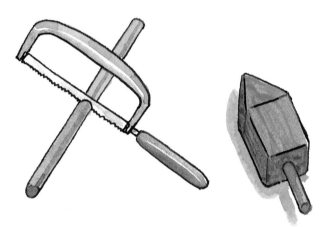

5 Cut a small length of thin dowel with a fretsaw and push the dowel into the dreidel. Leave it to dry until the clay is quite hard.

6 Paint the clay with acrylic paint and then draw on each face with a metallic pen. Brush on some clear varnish.

Dreidels have a special symbol written on each side, or you could draw shapes instead.

35

Star Bright

The Star of David is a lovely shape. You could make one for Hannukah or for Christmas.

1 Collect six ice-cream sticks or buy a packet from a craft shop. Paint each one with yellow or gold paint and leave them to dry.

2 Arrange three sticks in a triangle so that each stick has one end on top. Glue the joins.

36

3 Make a second triangle in the same way. Lay the two triangles side by side and put a stack of books on top until the glue dries.

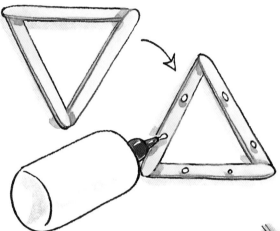

4 Arrange the two triangles so that all six points are the same size. Glue the joins and put the books on top again.

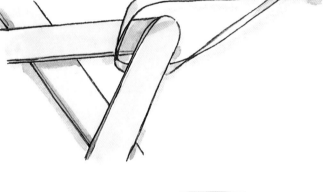

5 Tie a loop of narrow ribbon or string through one of the points so that you can hang the decoration.

Hang the star in a window or at the top of the Christmas tree.

Sweet Wreath

The difficult part in this project will be not eating the sweets until Christmas!

1 Cut a large hole in the middle of a paper plate. Lay it on another plate and mark around the hole in pencil, then cut the second plate along the pencil lines.

2 Put glue around the rim of one paper plate and stick the other one on top. Let the glue dry.

3 Cut a wide strip of green crêpe paper. Tape one end on the wreath base and carefully wind it around to cover the plates. Tape down the end.

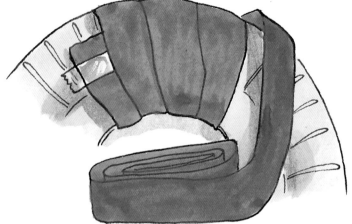

38

4 Cut a narrow strip of red crêpe paper and wind it around as shown. Tape both ends at the back of the wreath.

5 Glue some wrapped sweets on the front of the wreath.

You might want to add a crêpe bow plus a loop of string for hanging your wreath.

Dear Reindeer

Rudolf may have had
a red nose but with a bit of work
you can have red antlers!

1 Draw one antler shape on
scrap paper by copying the
picture on the next page. Cut out
the paper shape.

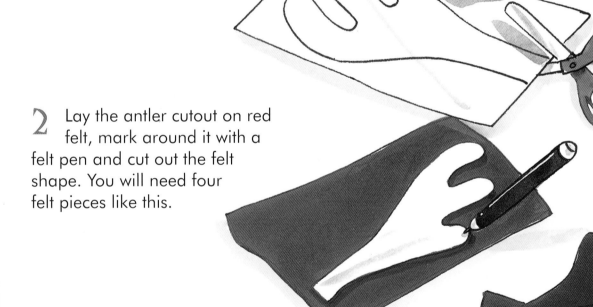

2 Lay the antler cutout on red
felt, mark around it with a
felt pen and cut out the felt
shape. You will need four
felt pieces like this.

3 Cut two long strips of stiff
card. Bend each strip twice
near the middle and glue the
ends together as shown.

40

4 Glue each card strip between two of the felt pieces.

5 Tape the strips onto the headband as shown. Cover the headband by winding a ribbon or strips of felt around it and gluing the ends in place.

Now go jingle those bells!

Tree Baubles

Make your own sparkling
decorations for the
Christmas tree.

YOU WILL NEED

a small jar
thin white card
a pencil
scissors
paper clips
PVA glue
tissue paper
clear varnish
a paintbrush
shiny scraps
narrow ribbon

1 Place a small jar on thin
card and draw around it.
Cut out two card circles
for each decoration.

2 Lay a paper clip so
that it juts out over
a card shape and glue
another shape on top.
Put some heavy books on
top until the glue is dry.

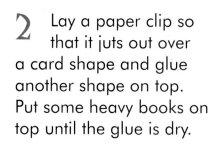

42

3 Tear small squares of tissue paper
  and glue them on the bauble,
folding them around the edges.
When both sides are covered,
brush on some clear varnish.

4 Glue on sequins, stickers or
  scraps of sweet wrappers.

5 Thread some narrow
  ribbon through the paper
clip and knot the ends to make
a hanging loop.

Make a whole set
while you have all
the stuff handy!

43

Super Santa

Santa and his elves would look
very festive on the mantelpiece
or on the Christmas table.

YOU WILL NEED

cardboard tubes
coloured paper
compasses
a pencil
black card
scissors
glue
cotton wool
plasticine

1 Wrap coloured paper around
a tube and glue down the
overlap. Set compasses 6.5 cm
apart and draw a circle on
coloured paper then cut it out.

2 Cut the circle in two and roll
one half into a cone. Glue
along the overlap and then glue
the cone onto the tube.

3 Glue a wisp of cotton wool
around the bottom of the cone
and a small ball on top. Stick a large
cotton ball onto the tube as a beard.

44

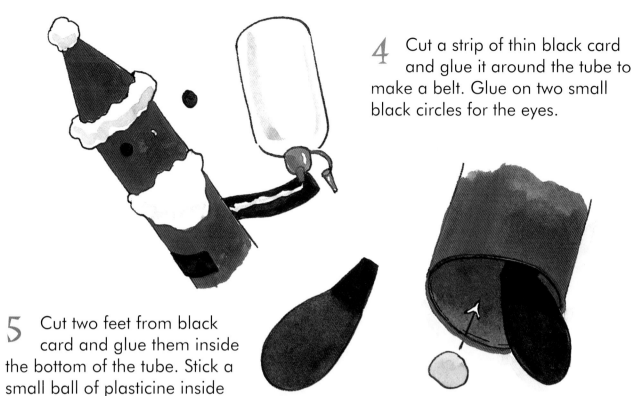

4   Cut a strip of thin black card and glue it around the tube to make a belt. Glue on two small black circles for the eyes.

5   Cut two feet from black card and glue them inside the bottom of the tube. Stick a small ball of plasticine inside the tube for balance.

The elves don't need any cotton wool but they do have pointy ears which have been stuck on.

Kwanzaa Beads

Red, green and black are the colours of the African celebration Kwanzaa. Why not make some beads as a gift for a friend?

YOU WILL NEED

paper
felt pens
a ruler
a pencil
scissors
a glue stick
string or cord

1 Cover a sheet of paper using red, green and black felt pens.

2 On the back of the paper, rule up lines which are wider at one end than at the other. Cut up the strips.

3 Put some glue on the narrow end of a strip, on the blank side of the paper.

46

4 Lay the wide end of the strip along a pencil. Turn it so that the strip is rolled around and then press the end down firmly.

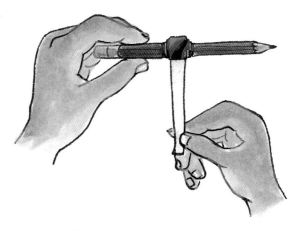

5 Slide the bead off the pencil and make some more. Thread the beads onto a length of cord and knot the ends to make a necklace.

The small beads are made with strips of coloured paper that are the same width all the way along.

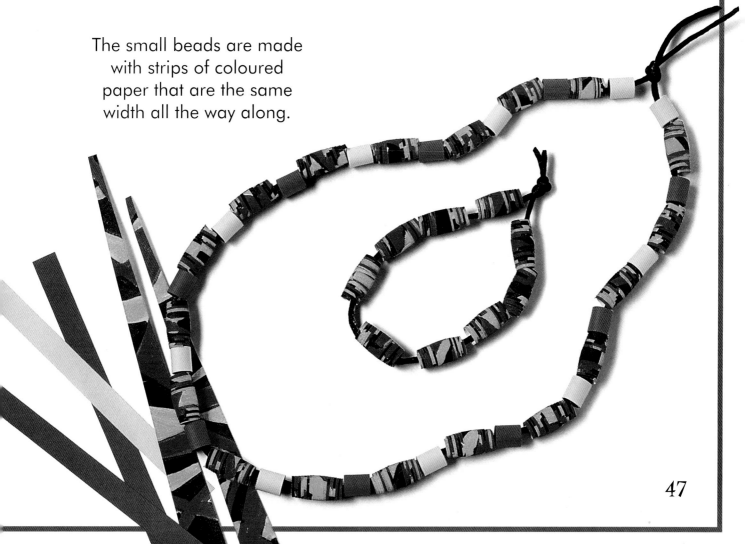

Index